peak one part 2

Alan Brighouse
David Godber
Peter Patilla

(relating to National Curriculum Levels 3 and 4)

Nelson

Thomas Nelson and Sons Ltd
Nelson House   Mayfield Road
Walton-on-Thames   Surrey
KT12 5PL   UK

51 York Place
Edinburgh EH1 3JD   UK

Thomas Nelson (Hong Kong) Ltd
Toppan Building 10/F   22A Westlands Road
Quarry Bay   Hong Kong

Distributed in Australia by

Thomas Nelson Australia
102 Dodds Street
South Melbourne   Victoria 3205

Nelson Canada
1120 Birchmount Road
Scarborough   Ontario
M1K 5G4   Canada

© **A. Brighouse, D. Godber, P. Patilla 1981, 1989**

Original edition 1981
This edition first published 1989

ISBN 0-17-421559-2
NPN 9 8 7 6 5 4 3

Printed in Hong Kong

Filmset in Nelson Teaching Alphabet
by Mould Type Foundry Ltd
Dunkirk Lane   Leyland   England

Design   Sharon Platt, Linda Reed

Photography   Chris Ridgers

Illustration   Anne Axworthy, Simon Stern, Taurus Graphics

Cover illustration   Mathew Bell

Photographic props courtesy of E J Arnold Ltd, Hestair Hope Ltd

The authors and publishers would like to thank the headmaster, teachers and pupils of Granard Junior School, Putney where photographs were taken.

Contents

Number and Algebra

This is an **add** machine.

It adds 4 to any number.

Copy and complete this table.

1.

IN	7	3	5	12	16	9	8	17	15	19
OUT	11									

The machine now adds 7.

Copy and complete this table.

2.

IN	5	9	15	8	20	17	11	18	23	19
OUT	12									

1. Which answers are even numbers?

2. Which answers have a zero in them?

3. Which answers are greater than 100?

4. In which sums did the units have to be changed for a ten?

A
```
    4 2
  + 2 8
  _____

  _____
```

B
```
    1 7
  + 8 2
  _____

  _____
```

C
```
    5 7
  + 6 2
  _____

  _____
```

D
```
    3 9
  + 4 3
  _____

  _____
```

E
```
    1 4
  + 7 3
  _____

  _____
```

F
```
    6 5
  + 2 5
  _____

  _____
```

G
```
    1 3
  + 2 4
  _____

  _____
```

H
```
    4 7
  + 1 6
  _____

  _____
```

I
```
    1 5
  + 9 6
  _____

  _____
```

J
```
    4 7
  + 3 3
  _____

  _____
```

K
```
    1 3
  + 3 8
  _____

  _____
```

L
```
    5 2
  + 1 6
  _____

  _____
```

M
```
    4 6
    7 3
  + 1 3
  _____

  _____
```

N
```
    2 9
    3 8
  + 1 7
  _____

  _____
```

O
```
    7 4
    1 2
  + 2 5
  _____

  _____
```

P
```
    3 9
    6 4
  + 2 6
  _____

  _____
```

5

Rod abacus, beads

Begin with this number each time.

1. Make it twenty more.

2. Make it fifty more.

3. Make it three hundred more.

4. Make it one hundred more.

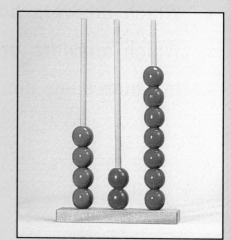

Begin with this number each time.

5. Make it ten less.

6. Make it thirty less.

7. Make it four hundred less.

8. Make it six hundred less.

Begin with this number each time.

9. Make it 4 more.

10. Make it 5 more.

11. Make it 30 more.

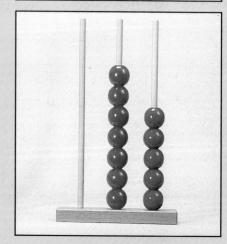

How many different ways can you get an answer of 7?

$$
\begin{array}{r} 3 \\ +4 \\ \hline \end{array}
\qquad
\begin{array}{r} 2 \\ 3 \\ +2 \\ \hline \end{array}
\qquad
\begin{array}{r} 9 \\ -2 \\ \hline \end{array}
$$

One way is by adding 2 numbers.

Another way is by adding 3 numbers.

Another way is by subtracting
one number from another.

Now find as many different ways
as you can.
Give one example of each way
you find.

Calculator

Which answer has no sum?

sums	answers
	93
47 + 36	132
59 + 61	83
27 + 75	107
69 + 37	127
54 + 39	120
94 + 36	102
87 + 45	145
28 + 58	86
77 + 68	130
40 + 67	106

Write a sum to match the answer.

Digit cards 0 to 9

Use the digit cards 0 to 9.
Each digit has a home.

☐ + ☐ = 11

☐ + ☐ = 8

☐ + 5 = 9

3 + ☐ = 5

☐ + ☐ = 10

☐ + ☐ = 10

Mr. Porter works at a railway station.
He sells railway tickets.
Here is a list of tickets he sold one week.

Day	To Nottingham	To Leicester	To London
Monday	37	11	64
Tuesday	31	13	56
Wednesday	53	14	63
Thursday	23	16	107
Friday	47	26	73
Saturday	69	32	143

1. How many tickets did he sell each day?

2. On which day did he sell the fewest tickets?

3. On which day did he sell most tickets?

4. How many more people went to London than Leicester on Saturday?

5. How many more people went to London than Nottingham on Saturday?

6. How many more tickets did he sell on Saturday than on Friday?

7. How many tickets to Nottingham did he sell that week?

8. How many tickets to Leicester did he sell that week?

9. How many tickets to London did he sell that week?

10. How many tickets did he sell altogether that week?

Which numbers do the letters point to?

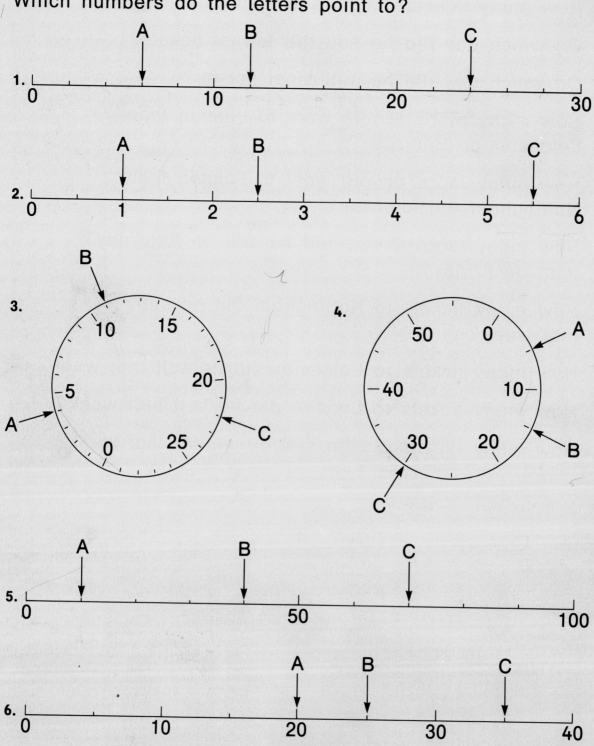

Measures

How long?

1.

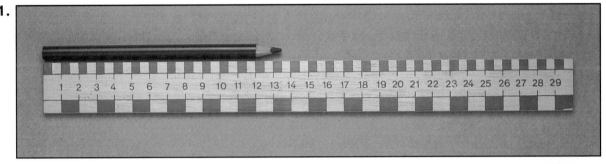

How heavy?

2.

3.

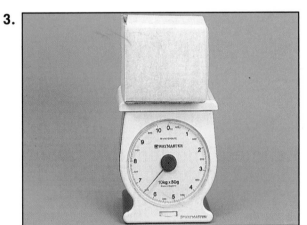

How many ml of water?

4.

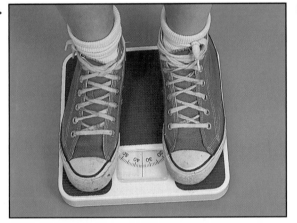

5.

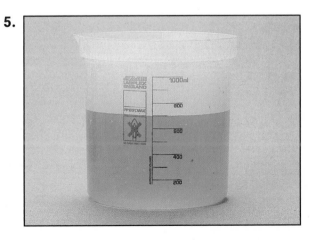

Tape measure, chalk

Remember: a sensible guess is called an **estimate.**

Estimate the length of your span.

Now measure your span.

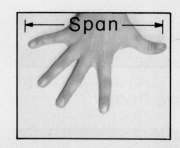

Estimate the length of your stride.

Now measure your stride.

14

1. How many cm in 1 metre?

2. How many cm in $\frac{1}{2}$ metre?

3. How many cm in $1\frac{1}{2}$ metres?

4. How many cm in 3 metres?

Make each of these up to 1 metre.
What must be added?

5. 55 cm   6. 86 cm   7. 43 cm

8. 62 cm   9. 19 cm   10. 75 cm

Measure these lines.

11. _____

12. _____

13. _____

14. _____

15. _____

16. _____

17. _____

18. _____

19. _____

20. _____

Bow calipers, metre stick

You will need a friend to help you.
Use bow calipers.
Measure these parts of your body.

Bow calipers, ruler

The distance across a circle is called the **diameter**.

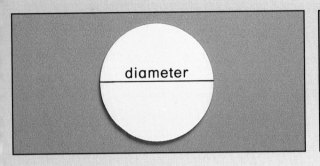

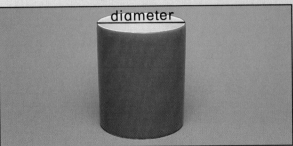

Measure the diameter of objects like these.

2 dice

Start

$$50$$

Throw 2 dice

Subtract the total.

$$41$$

Throw again

Subtract the total.

$$29$$

Next throw

Subtract the total.

$$18$$

Next throw

Subtract the total.

$$8$$

Next throw

Subtract the total.

$$0$$

Now you play the game.
How many throws did you need to reach 0?

Counters

Find pairs of numbers with a difference of 80.
Cover the pairs with counters.

552	216	307	493
148	437	472	227
337	413	227	68
136	357	267	147

Which numbers have not been covered?
Write a partner for each number.

Base 10 apparatus, place value sheet

Subtract 172 from each of these numbers.

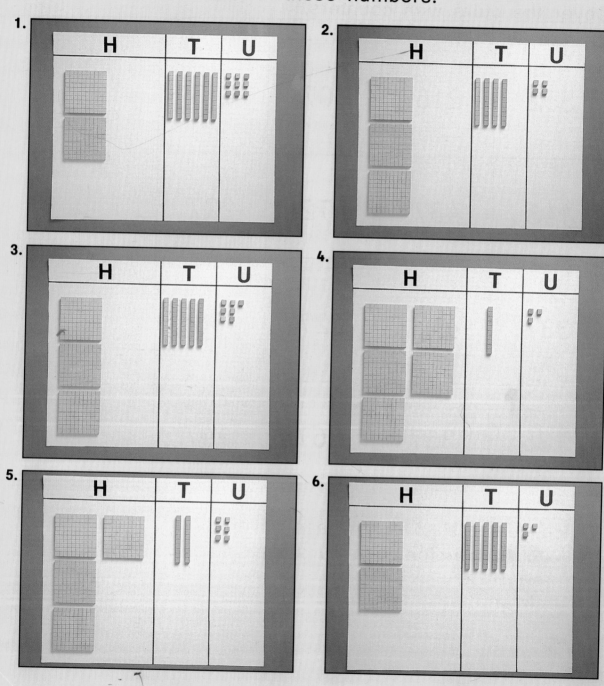

Base 10 apparatus, place value sheet

1.
```
  8 1 1
- 6 8 6
```

2.
```
  5 2 1
- 1 3 4
```

3.
```
  6 7 5
- 3 8 8
```

4.
```
  5 2 1
- 2 5 4
```

5.
```
  9 3 3
- 4 6 4
```

6.
```
  8 7 0
- 6 8 3
```

7.
```
  7 2 1
- 5 7 6
```

8.
```
  3 6 3
- 1 7 4
```

9.
```
  4 7 6
- 2 9 8
```

10.
```
  5 3 4
-   7 6
```

11.
```
  6 2 0
- 4 5 6
```

12.
```
  3 1 5
- 1 7 6
```

13. Subtract 139 from 524.

14. What is the difference between 89 and 213?

15. From 436 take 192.

16. How much greater than 246 is 431?

17. How many less than 642 is 294?

18. Take 175 from 421.

19. 425 − 132

20. 714 − 426

21. 647 − 329

22. 521 − 264

23. 611 − 208

24. 420 − 287

25. 821 − 642

26. 913 − 564

27. 584 − 399

Base 10 apparatus, place value sheet

Put 204 on your place value sheet.

Subtract 167.

```
    2 0 4
  - 1 6 7
  _____

  _____
```

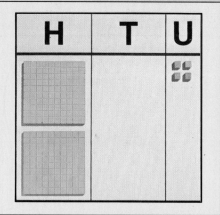

There are no tens to change into units.

Change a hundred into tens.

Now change a ten into units.

Subtract 167.

How many are left?

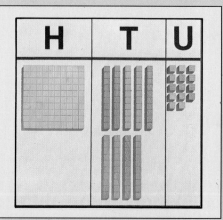

Subtract 167 from each of these.

1.

H		T	U

2.

H		T	U

3.

H		T	U

Base 10 apparatus, place value sheet

1.
```
   4 0 0
 - 1 1 3
 _____
```

2.
```
   5 0 4
 - 3 4 7
 _____
```

3.
```
   4 0 6
 - 1 8 8
 _____
```

4.
```
   6 0 0
 -   6 4
 _____
```

5.
```
   5 0 1
 - 3 2 2
 _____
```

6.
```
   5 0 7
 - 4 6 8
 _____
```

7.
```
   7 0 0
 - 1 7 7
 _____
```

8.
```
   4 0 3
 - 2 4 5
 _____
```

9.
```
   8 0 3
 - 5 1 4
 _____
```

10.
```
   7 0 5
 - 3 9 9
 _____
```

11.
```
   7 0 8
 - 5 7 8
 _____
```

12.
```
   9 0 0
 - 3 2 6
 _____
```

13.
```
   8 0 1
 - 7 6 5
 _____
```

14.
```
   6 0 3
 - 4 4 4
 _____
```

15.
```
   9 0 4
 - 8 2 5
 _____
```

16.
```
   8 0 7
 -   6 8
 _____
```

17.
```
   8 0 0
 - 6 4 3
 _____
```

18.
```
   9 0 6
 - 3 4 9
 _____
```

19.
```
   6 0 8
 - 2 1 7
 _____
```

20.
```
   7 0 3
 - 4 6 5
 _____
```

Calculator

Numbers which follow each other are called **consecutive numbers**.

13 and 14 are a pair of consecutive numbers.

Find each pair of consecutive numbers.

1. $173 - \boxed{} - \boxed{} = 100$

2. $45 + \boxed{} + \boxed{} = 100$

3. $15 + \boxed{} + \boxed{} = 100$

4. $207 - \boxed{} - \boxed{} = 100$

5. $61 + \boxed{} + \boxed{} = 100$

6. $179 - \boxed{} - \boxed{} = 100$

Calculator

Choose the estimate you think is nearest to the answer.
Use the calculator to check.

1. $242 + 84$

2. $527 - 237$

3. $472 - 284$

4. $153 + 255$

5. $317 - 198$

6. $194 + 195$

7. $114 + 95$

8. $283 - 179$

9. $564 - 273$

10. $143 + 268$

estimate

| 100 | 200 | 300 | 400 |

Plasticine, straws

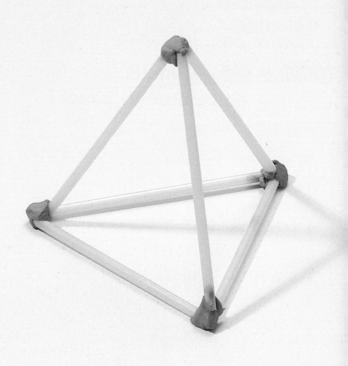

Make a tetrahedron from 4 plasticine corners and 6 straws.

Make a cube using plasticine corners and straws.
How many plasticine corners and straws do you need?

Use the glossary to find another name for a corner.
Make other shapes with straws and plasticine corners.

This triangular prism has 5 faces.
The faces are triangles and rectangles.

How many faces has each of these?
What shapes are they?

1.

2.

3.

4.

5. How many edges has each shape?

Plane shapes

A 4-sided shape is called a **quadrilateral**.

Put each pair of triangles together to make quadrilaterals.

Some of the quadrilaterals you made have special names.
Can you name them?
The glossary will help you.

Plane shapes

Here are some polygons.
Use the glossary to find their names.

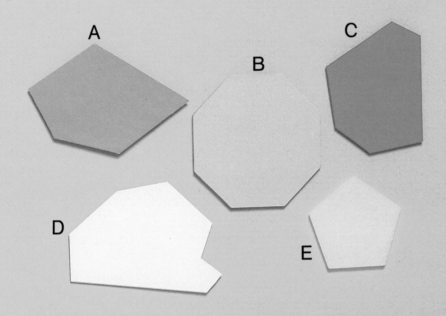

A   B   C

D   E

A diagonal goes across
a shape from one vertex
to another.

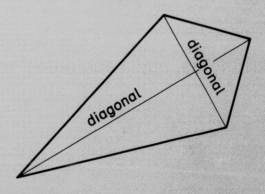

Draw a hexagon.
Draw all its diagonals.

Plane shapes

These patterns have been made from rectangles and squares.

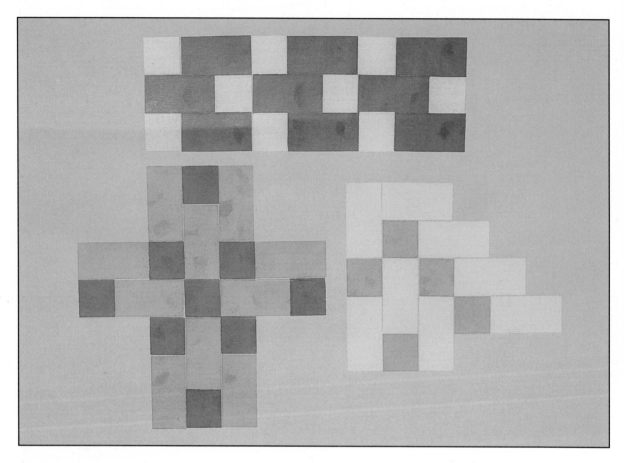

Use triangles and rectangles to make patterns.

Coloured cubes

Use two red cubes
   two green cubes
   two blue cubes
   two yellow cubes.

Make a cube so that each
face shows all four colours.

Make these shapes from 8 cubes.

9 pin geoboard, elastic bands, spotty paper

Stretch an elastic band between
any 2 pins.
The elastic band must be in a
straight line.

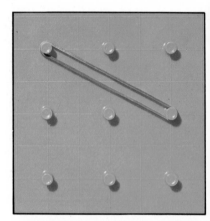

Stretch other elastic bands between
2 pins.
They must all stretch the same
distance as the first one.
How many elastic bands did you
put on your geoboard?

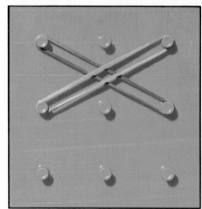

Repeat this choosing a different distance between 2 pins.

How many different distances can you find between
2 pins?

9 pin geoboard, elastic bands, spotty paper

How many squares can you make on your geoboard?
Here are a few.

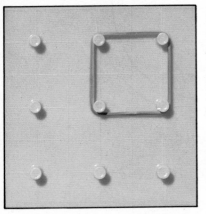 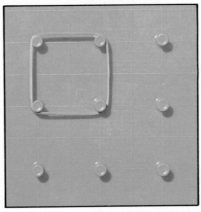 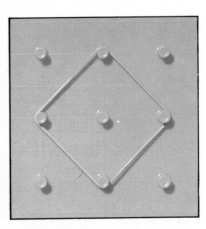

How many different squares can you make?
Each square must be different in size.

Record your results on spotty paper.
Arrange the results in order of size.

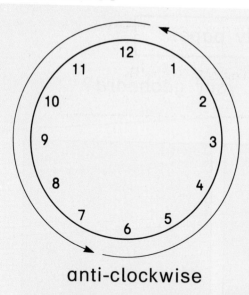

anti-clockwise

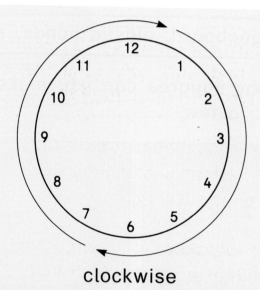

clockwise

In which direction would you turn each of these?

1.

turn the tap off

2.

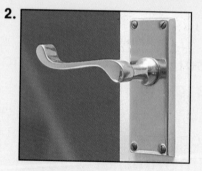

open the door

3.

take the cap
off the bottle

4.

turn the
volume up

5.

take the screw
out of the wood

6.

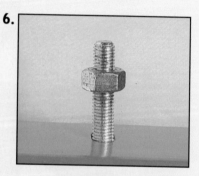

tighten the nut

Stand up and face the blackboard.
Turn round until you face the blackboard again.
You have turned a full turn.

Face the blackboard again.
Make a half turn clockwise.
What are you facing?

Face the blackboard again.
Make a quarter turn clockwise.
What are you facing?

Face the blackboard again.
Make a quarter turn anti-clockwise.
What are you facing?

Number and Algebra

Grouping 16

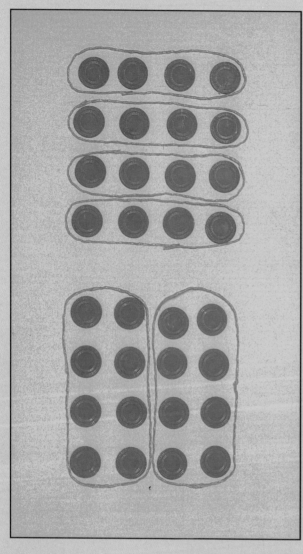

4 in each group

4 groups

4 × 4 = 16

8 in each group

2 groups

8 × 2 = 16

Can you find another way to group 16?

Group each of these in as many ways as you can.
  12   18   24

Complete these.

×	1	2	3	4	5	6	7	8	9	10
3										
6										
9										

×	1	2	3	4	5	6	7	8	9	10
2										
4										
8										

×	1	2	3	4	5	6	7	8	9	10
5										
7										
10										

37

Find the total of each crate.

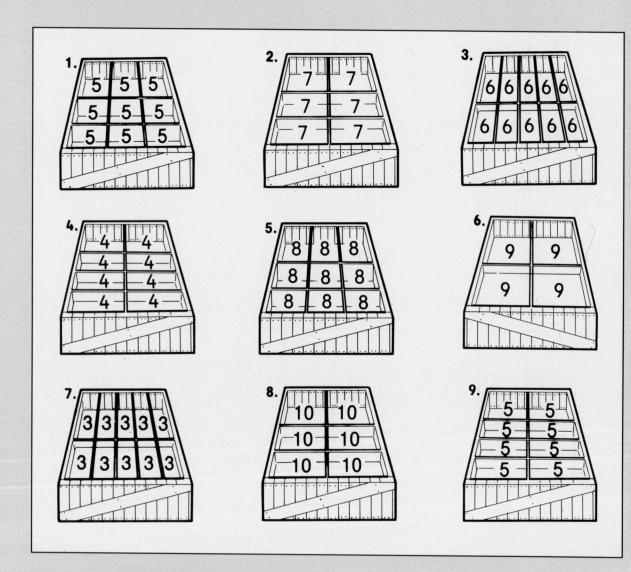

Now do these.

10. 5×8 11. 3×2 12. 4×7 13. 9×5

14. 3×8 15. 6×6 16. 7×6 17. 5×7

18. 10×5 19. 8×4 20. 3×9 21. 9×4

Calculator

Multiply these numbers by 10.
You can use a calculator.

15   22   17   30   57

What do you notice?

Multiply each of these by 10.
Can you do it without using a calculator?

42   67   33   52   87   92   73

Multiply each of these by 7.
You can use a calculator.

20   30   40   50   60   70

Now multiply the same numbers by 6.
Can you do it without using a calculator?

Base 10 apparatus

Multiply each of these by 2.

1.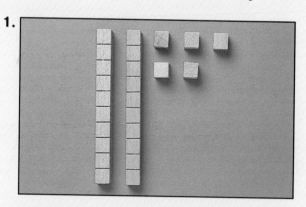

2.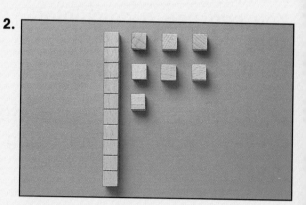

Multiply each of these by 4.

3.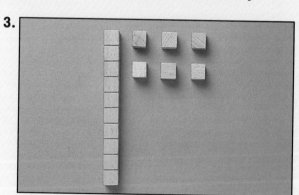

4.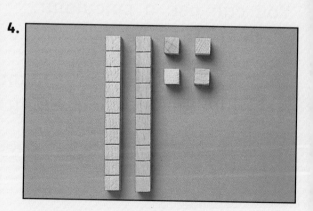

Multiply each of these by 5.

5.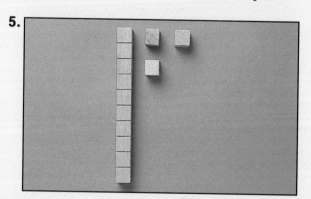

6.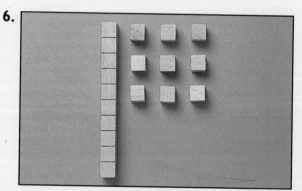

Find the missing numbers.

1.

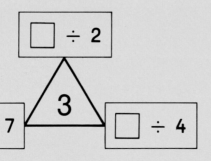

2.

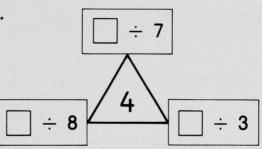

3.

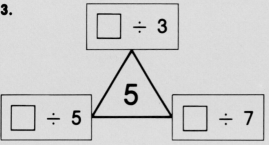

4.

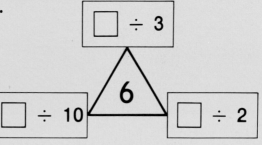

5.

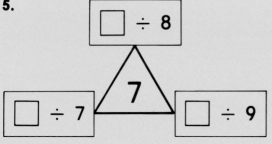

6.

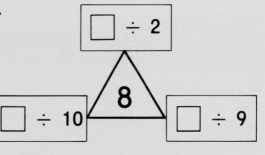

7.

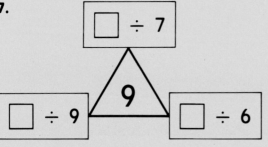

8.

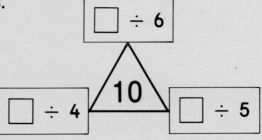

Money

Find the change from 50p.

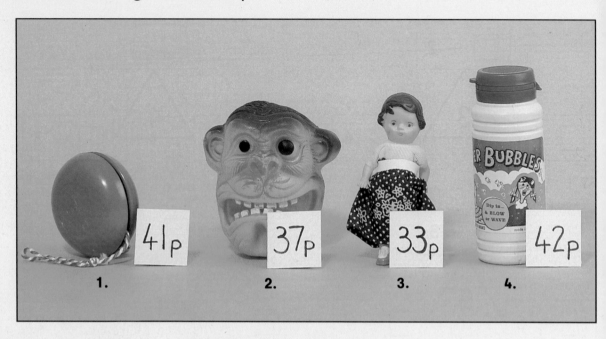

1. 41p   2. 37p   3. 33p   4. 42p

Each of these is change from £1.
How much was spent each time?

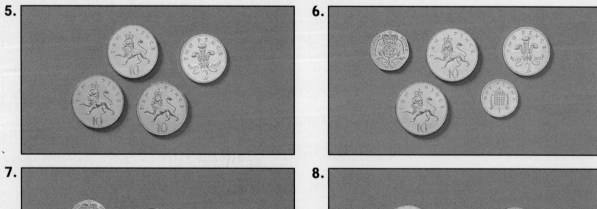

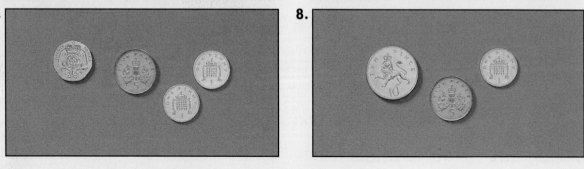

5.   6.   7.   8.

How many of each can you buy for £1.

1. 22ᵖ

2. NOTE BOOK 50 SHEETS RULED 33p

3. Britvic CITRUS SPRING SPARKLING ORANGE DRINK 45p

4. CHERRYADE Carters 27p

5. 18p

6. 12p

Which gives 4p change?

Small cornet 30p
Large cornet 45p
Ice lolly 25p
Ice-cream flake 55p
Choc ice 40p
Ice-cream tub 50p

1. What is the cost of an ice-cream tub and a large cornet?

2. Which 3 items together cost £1.

3. You buy a small cornet.
   You give the ice-cream man 50p.
   You are given three coins as change.
   What are the coins?

4. You buy a choc ice.
   Which silver coins could you give the ice-cream man?

Money

This can be written as £1·05.

This can be written as £1·32.

Write these in the same way.

1.

2.

3.

4.

5.

6.

Measures

Clock stamp

Write the times these clocks show.

1.
2.
3.
4.

Stamp 6 clock faces.
Make the clocks show these times:

5. 4.20

6. 3.45

7. 8.15

8. 9.50

9. 6.05

10. 10.35

60 minutes = 1 hour

This clock shows 5 o'clock.

Write the time it will be:

11. 5 minutes later.

12. 15 minutes later.

13. 30 minutes later.

14. 40 minutes later.

15. 50 minutes later.

16. 1 hour later.

Jill asked her friends which pets they had.

She made a table of the information.

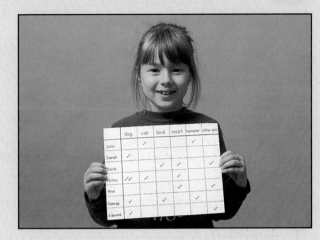

	dog	cat	bird	rabbit	hamster	other pet
John		✓			✓	
Sarah	✓					
Kalid			✓	✓		✓
Mieko	✓✓	✓		✓		
Ann				✓		✓
George	✓		✓		✓	
Edward	✓					✓

1. Who had the most pets?

2. Which pet was the most popular?

Make a table to show the pets your friends have.

Assessment

1.
$$347$$
$$+ 186$$
_____

2. Make this number 30 bigger.

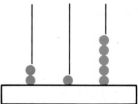

3. Which numbers do the letters point to?

4. What must be added to 65 cm to make 1 metre?

5. Measure the diameter of this circle.

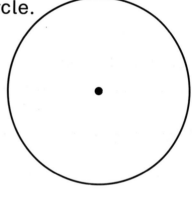

6.
$$428$$
$$- 154$$
_____

7.
$$304$$
$$- 197$$
_____

Name these shapes.

8.

9.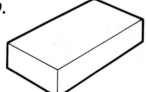

10.

11.
$$18 \times 4$$

12.
$$13 \times 9$$

13. $2 \overline{)56}$

14. $3 \overline{)67}$

15. What fraction is shaded?

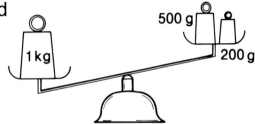

16. What weight must be added to balance the kilogram?

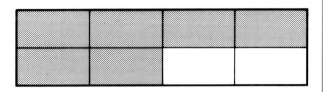

17. You spend 74p.
How much change from £1?

18. Show the time 35 minutes later.

   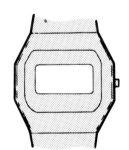

19. $\frac{1}{2} + \frac{1}{4} =$

20. $\frac{\square}{4} = \frac{1}{2}$

Glossary

abacus

anti-clockwise

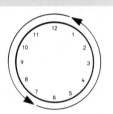

bow calipers

a measuring instrument

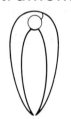

clockwise

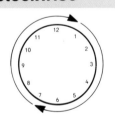

column graph

cone

consecutive numbers

'next door' numbers (e.g. 22, 23, 24)

cube

cuboid

cylinder

diagonal

a line going across a shape from one vertex to another

diameter

a straight line through the centre of a circle

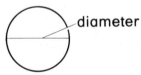

digit

single number (from 0 to 9)

digit cards

cards showing single numbers

edge

a cube has 12 edges

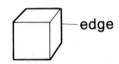

equilateral triangle

a triangle with 3 equal sides and 3 equal angles

estimate

a sensible guess

face

a cube has 6 faces

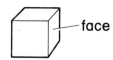

hexagon

any shape with 6 sides

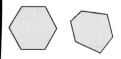

kilogram (kg)

a measure of weight
1 kg = 1000 g

kite

a special quadrilateral

octagon

any shape with 8 sides

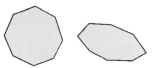

parallelogram

a special quadrilateral

pentagon

any shape with 5 sides

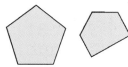

polygon

shape with many sides

pyramid

quadrilateral

any shape with 4 sides

remainder

the number left over when dividing

rhombus

a special quadrilateral

tetrahedron

a solid shape with four faces

triangular prism

vertex

a corner

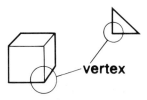

vertices

more than one vertex

71

Multiplication square

1	2	3	4	5	6	7	8	9	10
2	4	6	8	10	12	14	16	18	20
3	6	9	12	15	18	21	24	27	30
4	8	12	16	20	24	28	32	36	40
5	10	15	20	25	30	35	40	45	50
6	12	18	24	30	36	42	48	54	60
7	14	21	28	35	42	49	56	63	70
8	16	24	32	40	48	56	64	72	80
9	18	27	36	45	54	63	72	81	90
10	20	30	40	50	60	70	80	90	100